Lela and the Butterflies

Sherri Maret

Written by Sherri and Tim Maret

Illustrated by Merisha Sequoia Clark

muddy boots

Guilford, Connecticut

An imprint of The Rowman & Littlefield Publishing Group, Inc.
4501 Forbes Blvd., Ste. 200
Lanham, MD 20706
www.rowman.com

MuddyBootsBooks.com

Distributed by NATIONAL BOOK NETWORK

Text copyright © 2020 by Sherri Maret and Tim Maret
Illustrations copyright © 2020 by Merisha Sequoia Clark
Book design by Amanda Wilson

British Library Cataloguing in Publication Information available

Library of Congress Control Number: 2020933903

ISBN 978-1-63076-382-4 (hardcover : alk. paper)
ISBN 978-1-63076-383-1 (electronic)

Printed in Johor Bahru, Malaysia, May 2020

Lela loved butterflies.

She had butterflies practically everywhere.

When Lela heard about a **butterfly walk**, she wanted to go. Her parents were happy to take her.

Ranger Maggie greeted everyone before
leading them down a path that wound
through a meadow full of **native flowers**
and **flitting butterflies**.

"Butterflies and wildflowers need each other. The **butterflies drink nectar** from the flowers and in return they pollinate the flowers so that the plants can make seeds," Ranger Maggie explained.

"Wow! What kind is that?" asked a boy.

"It's a **silver-spotted skipper.** You can see why it's called that because of the silvery spot on its hindwings."

"There's a monarch!" Lela exclaimed.

Ranger Maggie smiled at Lela's excitement. "Did you know that you can tell the male and female monarch apart? The males have a small black spot on each of their hindwings. In addition to being beautiful, monarchs are amazing long-distance flyers. In the fall, they will begin their journey south to Mexico."

"Monarchs are my favorite butterflies," Lela told Ranger Maggie.

"They're mine, too, but don't tell the other butterflies," Ranger Maggie whispered, which made Lela giggle.

They stopped at a patch of bushy plants covered in pink flowers. "These plants are called swamp milkweed and they are a favorite food for monarch caterpillars. Although milkweed plants are poisonous to most animals, they are delicious to monarchs. **Can anyone find a caterpillar?**"

Lela could see where caterpillars had chewed on leaves but she couldn't find any caterpillars. Finally, Lela's mom said, "I found one." Everyone gathered around to see. Lela soon found one, too.

Ranger Maggie pointed to another butterfly flitting ahead of them. **"Look everyone! There goes a black swallowtail butterfly."** The swallowtail landed on a flower and started to drink nectar. "Most adult butterflies will drink nectar from many different flowers. Caterpillars are picky about what they eat and will often eat only one type of plant. Black swallowtail caterpillars like to eat parsley and dill, which are commonly grown in herb gardens."

Towards the end of the walk, Ranger Maggie gathered her group together. "There aren't as many meadows and wildflowers as there used to be, which means fewer places for the butterflies to thrive and less food for them to eat. One way to help butterflies is to plant a butterfly garden like the one here at the nature center. You can pick up an information sheet on how to do that at the nature desk."

"Can we plant a butterfly garden?" asked Lela.

"If you'll help with making the garden and maintaining it," replied her father.

The man at the nature desk said, "Plant the seeds in the fall because many seeds need a winter's chill to grow in the spring. Good luck with your garden!"

In the fall, Lela and her father looked for a place to put the garden.

"I think this corner will work well because it gets a lot of sun," said Lela's father. They dug up the grass and mixed in some compost to enrich the soil. Lela scattered the seeds and then raked them into the earth.

When spring arrived, Lela was excited to see tiny plants had sprouted! As the weather warmed, Lela watered when the soil got too dry and the plants grew taller and taller. By summer, a few plants had begun to bloom.

"Hello butterflies. Welcome to my garden!" Lela was happy to discover a few small swamp milkweed plants growing among the other flowers. While she saw many different butterflies, Lela waited patiently for a monarch to visit.

Weeks passed and the swamp milkweed plants grew larger.

"There's a monarch in the garden!" Lela called to her parents. They watched it drink nectar from one of the flowers.

Later Lela found a couple of white balls on the undersides of the milkweed leaves. Monarch eggs!

Lela checked the garden waiting to see caterpillars. When she saw small rice-sized caterpillars, she knew the eggs had hatched. The caterpillars ate milkweed leaves and grew every day.

"Where did the caterpillars go?" Lela asked her mother. "There is only this one left."

"I remember reading that monarch caterpillars often crawl away to a safe place when they are ready to make a chrysalis and transform into a butterfly," replied her mother. "Remember? It was in one of your books."

"That's right. I forgot."

Lela searched around until she found a bright green chrysalis attached to a sunflower plant. Several days later she could see the orange and black stripes of the developing butterfly inside.

"Mom! Dad! The chrysalis is empty!" Nearby a monarch butterfly sat on a sunflower drying its wings. Once its wings dried, the butterfly joined the other butterflies sipping nectar in Lela's garden.

That fall, after the flowers had turned brown, Lela and her father gathered up the flower seeds. Lela carefully split open the seed pods of the milkweed plants to get the seeds that were inside. They cleared a new section of ground to make room for the **butterfly garden** to expand and carefully raked some of the seeds into the soil.

Lela had a lot of seeds left over. She thought about what she could do to help the butterflies.

"Ms. Hower, I have all of these seeds from my butterfly garden. **Do you think we could make a garden here at school?**" Ms. Hower liked Lela's idea, and soon the students were busy clearing ground and raking in the seeds at the edge of the school yard.

Lela still had some leftover seeds so she **planted them in little pots** and put them in the garage where they would be chilled over the winter.

The next spring **Lela gave milkweed plants to friends, classmates, and neighbors** who wanted to help the monarchs. Lela also brought some milkweed plants to Ms. Sarah at the library and helped her plant a butterfly garden.

Lela's hard work was paying off. With every new butterfly garden, there was more habitat for many butterflies. Lela smiled as she thought about all the milkweed plants the monarchs would find when they arrived in the summer after the long flight from Mexico.

Lela loves butterflies.

She has butterflies practically
everywhere!

How to Grow a Butterfly Garden

1. Decide on the location and size of your garden. A sunny location is best, although most flowers can survive several hours of shade each day. If you start small, you can always expand later.

2. Clear the area of grass and weeds and prepare the soil by mixing in some compost or topsoil.

3. Choose the seeds to plant. A variety of different flowers is best. If you buy a commercial butterfly garden seed mix, make sure that many of the seeds are for native plants. Seed mixes often contain seeds for both annual and perennial plants. Many annual plants are good butterfly plants (especially cosmos and zinnias), but they die at the end of the season and need to be replanted every year. Perennial plants will live for many years. You will also want plants that bloom at different times so that butterflies can find nectar in spring, summer, and fall.

4. If you want to have caterpillars in your garden, you'll need to include host plants that the caterpillars eat. Each butterfly has its own host plant(s). Since monarch caterpillars only eat milkweed, be sure to plant some milkweed seeds or plants. If you plant some parsley or dill seeds, you might convince black swallowtail butterflies to lay eggs in your garden.

5. Scatter the seeds over the garden area and rake them gently into the soil. Seeds of many perennial plants, including milkweed, need a cold period in order to germinate and should be planted in the fall. Seeds of most annuals and some perennials can be planted in the spring. If you bought a seed mix, follow the instructions on the packet. Adding some live plants can jumpstart your garden. If you add live plants to your garden, springtime is best.

6. Take care of your garden. Young plants are tender and will need to be watered when the soil gets dry. Perennial plants will eventually grow deep roots, after which they won't need to be watered except during long dry spells. Weeds and grass will try to grow in your garden, so you should remove them while they are still small.

7. Your butterfly garden will attract pollinators other than butterflies. You are likely to get bees, moths, beetles, and maybe even hummingbirds. These species need our help, too, so please welcome them to your garden.

8. Harvest seeds from your plants in late summer and fall and divide large perennial plants in the spring or fall. Share with friends and family so they can plant their own butterfly gardens.

9. If you don't have space for a garden, you can still help butterflies by planting zinnias, cosmos, or other butterfly-friendly flowers in pots.

10. Enjoy the beautiful flowers and butterflies.

For more information:
The Xerces society (https://xerces.org) has guides to butterfly-friendly plants for every region of the country, including which species of milkweed to plant.